Zen

Judaism

also by David M. Bader

Haikus for Jews:
For You, a Little Wisdom

How to Be an Extremely Reform Jew

Harmony Books

New York

Zen
Judaism

For You, a Little Enlightenment

David M. Bader

Published by Harmony Books, New York, New York.
Member of the Crown Publishing Group, a division of Random House, Inc.
www.randomhouse.com

HARMONY BOOKS is a registered trademark and the Harmony Books colophon is a trademark of Random House, Inc.

Printed in the United States of America

Library of Congress Cataloging-in-Publication Data

Bader, David M.
    Zen Judaism: for you, a little enlightment/David M. Bader.
      p. cm.
    1. Jewish wit and humor. 2. Judaism—Relations—Buddhism—
Humor. 3. Buddhism—Relations—Judaism—Humor. I. Title.
    PN6231.J5 B233 2002
    818'.5402—dc21

                                2002024695

ISBN 0-609-61021-X

10 9 8 7 6 5

First Edition

Acknowledgments

The author thanks Jake Morrissey, Shaye Areheart, Sarah Silbert, and everyone else at Harmony Books; literary agents John Boswell and Patty Brown; and kibbitzing attorney-at-law Benjamin E. Rosenberg, Esq. He is also grateful to his parents, whose encouraging words ("If you're so 'enlightened,' why aren't you rich?") were a constant source of inspiration. All mistakes are the author's, but that doesn't necessarily make him a bad person.

Preface

few spiritual practices are more intriguing or elusive than those of Zen Judaism. A growing movement, it offers a unique way to follow in the footsteps of the Buddha, ideally without gaining quite so much weight. Its sacred teachings, combining ancient Eastern meditation techniques with traditional Jewish lower-back pain, are not easily mastered. And yet, properly understood, Zen Judaism is capable of bringing about an enlightenment experience so pure, so elevating, and so intense, you could *plotz.*

A Japanese term, *Zen* is the counterpart to the Chinese *Chan,* which in turn is the counterpart to the Sanskrit *Dhyana,* a word that means, roughly, "Zen." The practice of Zen Judaism dates back to the famous Gautama Buddha of the sixth century B.C., the name *Buddha* meaning "enlightened one" or "awakened one." He was also known as Siddhartha, after his real name, Sidney Arthur Buddha.

The Buddha's parents, Max and Helen, were an affluent Jewish couple in suburban Kapilavatthu. They were proud of young Sidney, whom they virtually worshiped. As their neighbors rolled their eyes, they would describe the miraculous, god-like powers of their "little Buddhaleh." It was said that when the infant Buddha took his first steps, lotus blossoms bloomed directly under his feet. It was also said that the neighbors politely asked the Buddhas to keep the boy out of their flower beds.

The Buddha's teachers predicted that he would one day be a great sage. The idea thrilled his parents, as long as he went to law school first. But Sidney Buddha had other plans. As a young man, weary of his comfortable life and troubled by the suffering he saw around him, he resolved to renounce all his possessions and become a mendicant monk.

"A monk?" his father asked. "Can you make a living at that?" He urged him to reconsider, offering to set him up in the family import/export business. The Buddha refused.

"It's a Zen thing," he explained to his baffled family.

"This is all your fault," his parents said to each other.

When his mother had finished sewing name tags into his saffron robes (telling him to "wear them in good health"), the Buddha left home to seek an end to all human suffering. Amazingly, he succeeded, and the solution, it turned out, required less equipment than one might expect. The Buddha found that, through meditation, it was possible to reach Nirvana—an escape from the endless, painful cycle of aging, disease, death, and rebirth. This realization came as the Buddha sat in the lotus position on the Immovable Spot under the Tree of Enlightenment for forty-nine days in a row, after which he enunciated the Four Noble Truths:

ONE: Life is suffering.

TWO: The cause of all suffering is selfish craving and attachment.

THREE: There is a way to end all suffering, which I am about to explain.

FOUR: I have no feeling in my legs.

The Buddha also enunciated the Eightfold Path, the Five Hindrances, the Ten Perfections, the Threefold Refuge, the Thirteen Austere Practices, and so on, quickly earning a reputation as a compulsive list-maker.

People began to make pilgrimages from far and wide to hear the insights of the Enlightened One. "Don't hang a new suit on a wire hanger," he would instruct. "Always use a table pad under a hot dish. Art and jewelry are probably not the best investment. Never, ever order the brisket in a Hindu restaurant."

Devoted followers transcribed the teachings of the Buddha onto palm leaves, in languages such as Pali and Sanskrit. In time these works were translated into many other tongues, including Chinese, Japanese, and Yiddish. Later they were scribbled onto legal pads with a dull pencil and photocopied over and over again until the machine ran out of toner. At some point, someone accidentally spilled coffee on them. The insights that have survived, then, are distilled from a long and rich spiritual legacy, influenced by Zen, Tao, lox, and a number of other Scrabble words.

As you peruse these teachings, do not be surprised if not every word seems to make sense. Beneath any superficial appearance of confusion there lies a hidden layer, much more profound, that is also completely mystifying. At least you tried. As the Buddha taught, all that really matters is that you live mindfully, practice loving-kindness to all sentient beings, and never shop for shoes by mail order. Also, avoid fried foods, stay out of the sun, and stop worrying so much. You'll give yourself an ulcer.

Zen

Judaism

If you wish to know The Way,

don't ask for directions. Argue.

21

To know the Buddha is the highest attainment. Second highest is to go to the same doctor as the Buddha.

Zen is an end in itself. Your only goal must be *mushotoku,* the goal of having no goals, of striving not to strive.

"How is it possible to strive to not have goals?" you might ask. "Isn't that itself a goal?"

Don't be a smart aleck. You should be as goal-less and lacking in purpose as your cousin, the successful one.

be here now. Be someplace else later. Is that so complicated?

Though only your skin, sinews, and bones remain, though your blood and flesh dry up and wither away, yet shall you meditate and not stir until you have attained full Enlightenment. But first, a little nosh.

To find the Buddha, look within.

Deep inside you are ten thousand flowers.

Each flower blossoms ten thousand times.

Each blossom has ten thousand petals.

You might want to see a specialist.

take only what is given. Own

nothing but your robes and an alms bowl.

Unless, of course, you have the closet space.

$a$ccept misfortune as a blessing.
Do not wish for perfect health or a life
without problems. What would you talk
about?

To study the Way of the Buddha is to study the self. To study the self is to forget the self. To forget the self is to experience the complete dropping away of body and mind. The difficult part is keeping body and mind off after you've dropped them. Many people gain back body, mind, and an additional fifteen pounds. You must then study the Way of Jenny Craig.

let your mind be as a floating cloud. Let your stillness be as the wooded glen. And sit up straight. You'll never meet the Buddha with posture like that.

be master of yourself in all things. This can be used to your advantage at tax time.

Seek out all true dharmas. Pursue all stuffed dermas.

learn of the pine from the pine.

Learn of the bamboo from the bamboo.

Learn of the kugel from the kugel.

let go of pride, ego, and opinions. Admit your errors and forgive those of others. Relinquishment will lead to calm and healing in your relationships. If that doesn't work, try small-claims court.

What is the sound of one hand clapping? How could the Buddha weigh four hundred pounds and still do yoga? What exactly is "stuffed *kishke*"?

Meditate mindfully. Transcend
all other concerns. Concentrate solely on
the attainment of clear vision. This can
be accomplished in less than an hour at
Cohen Fashion Optical. Also, for a limited
time, purchase a second pair of frames
at half price.

be aware of your body. Be aware of your perceptions. Keep in mind that not every physical sensation is a symptom of a terminal illness.

The Tao that can be named is not the eternal Tao. The eternal name of the Tao is actually Taostein, but no one talks about it.

The enlightened monk attains permanent liberation—Nirvana. The unenlightened returns again and again to the wheel of suffering. Infinite deaths, infinite rebirths, infinite circumcisions.

There is no escaping karma. In a previous life, you never called, you never wrote, you never visited. And whose fault was that?

*a*bandon false dichotomies.
There is no distinction between "self" and
"non-self," "interior" and "exterior." The
universe is one. You are all that there is.
Ask your mother.

When you play basketball,
be the ball. When you sit on the bench,
be the towels.

Unhappiness stems from not having what is desired, or from having what is not desired. This can be avoided by neither having nor desiring. You can also try to exchange what you have but do not desire for what you desire but do not have. This requires knowing what store it came from.

42
43

To depart is to arrive. To leave is to stay. To say good-bye is to begin a lengthy conversation at the front door.

form is emptiness, emptiness is form. Just minutes ago you had a hat; now it's gone, fleeting as a puff of smoke. Your hat was merely part of an endlessly moving stream, a great river of transient phenomena, rising and falling, coming to be and passing away. Same with your missing gloves, and no, they are not behind the couch. Everything is impermanent, even the theory of impermanence. This is why it is so important to stay on top of things.

The Torah says, "Love thy neighbor as thy self." The Buddha says there is no "self." So maybe you are off the hook.

If there is no self, whose arthritis

is this?

When you work, just work.
When you eat, just eat. When you send
out, just send out.

The Eightfold Way of the Buddha requires Right Understanding, Right Thought, Right Speech, Right Action, Right Livelihood, Right Effort, Right Mindfulness, Right Concentration, and Right Worship of Your Mother. Actually, that's nine, but is the last one really asking so much?

48

49

buying retail is not The Way. In shopping, as in kung fu, there are only two outcomes: victory or death. You must have the fury of the dragon, the stealth of the snake, and the patience of the white crane. When the right item appears on sale, make a swift, unflinching charge (MasterCard/ VISA/Amex). There are no returns.

those who know do not *kibbitz*.

Those who *kibbitz* do not know.

*e*nlightenment is a sudden, wordless understanding. Stop telling everyone already.

$b$reathe in. Breathe out. Breathe in. Breathe out. Forget this and attaining Enlightenment will be the least of your problems.

life is suffering. Following the
Eightfold Way brings about the cessation of
suffering. But where is it written that you
are supposed to be happy?

The path of Enlightenment begins with renunciation. When you come of age, depart from the home of your childhood like a swan abandoning a lake. Later you may return, like a swan that needs laundry done.

$p$ractice pure meditation—
shikantaza or "just sitting"—to discover
the true nature of reality. Through this
technique, in time, you may attain the
realization that the true nature of reality
is extremely uneventful.

*d*o not *kvetch*. Be a *kvetch*.

Become one with your whining.

bow and remove your shoes when entering a room with wall-to-wall carpeting. Foot odors? This is where incense comes in.

If you meet the Buddha on the path, show him the photos of the grandchildren.

Wherever you go, there you are.

Your luggage is another story.

Never go on a pilgrimage empty-handed. Bring a gift, and chant something polite. For example:

With humble awareness, I offer,
at the blessed lotus-like feet of the Great
            Buddha,
this marble cake, freshly baked, and so
            moist it's Nirvana—
well, okay, not literally. Try it! Just a
            teensy piece?

Seek not the outer enticements.
Dwell not in the inner strife. Try to find a
nice place in the suburbs with good schools.

don't be a backseat driver.

Instead, quietly recite mantras of protection.

For example: "You're going to get us

all killed."

take refuge in the Buddha.

Take refuge in the Dharma. Take refuge

in the condo.

Practicing Right Livelihood means earning a living in a manner that does not harm you or others. Do nothing unjust or dishonest. Avoid careers that involve killing. Find an occupation furthering of love and compassion. Ask about the health plan. No freelancing!

do not be discouraged by
wandering thoughts or daydreams. So you
sat in the lotus position for four hours
meditating about real estate. It happens.

make room for the spirit of the Buddha at your dinner table. At Passover, make room for the prophet Elijah, too. And that's it. Two invisible guests are enough.

Practice the "wall-gazing" meditation. Pick a spot on the wall and focus on it. Maintain complete silence. Do not budge or look away. The sixth-century Zen master Bodhidharma once sat facing a wall for nine years perfecting his Enlightenment. See if you can hold out until the person arguing with you apologizes.

Whenever you feel anger, you should say, "May I be free of this anger!" This rarely works, but talking to yourself in public will encourage others to leave you alone.

Praising one's spouse every day will add to his or her happiness and long life. But who wants to live forever with an egomaniac?

drink tea and nourish life.
With the first sip, joy. With the second,
satisfaction. With the third, Danish.

be a radiant channel of light and love. Project compassionate acceptance and encouragement in all directions. Keep telling others, "May you be happy, may you be peaceful, may you be free from suffering. May all beings be happy, may all beings be peaceful, may all beings be free from suffering." Don't expect anyone to thank you for all your trouble.

One may vow to master the Dharma. One may even take a vow of celibacy. A vow of silence is out of the question.

*d*o not let children play contact sports like football. These only lead to injuries and instill a violent, war-like nature. Encourage your child to play peaceful games, like "sports doctor."

If you practice Zen meditation for long periods of time, you may be criticized by friends and relatives who feel you are shutting them out. Ignore these people.

What use is profit? Can accumulating money day after day in a trade or business truly bring satisfaction? Of course not. For that, one must go shopping.

$a$ttaining Nirvana can take eons.
One might have to make countless journeys
through the karmic cycle of birth, suffering,
death, and rebirth. You should only live
so long.

$d$eath comes to us all. Prepare
yourself by composing a "death poem," an
ancient practice of the Japanese Zen masters.
Your poem need not be morbid or self-
pitying, even as it captures the fleetingness
of human existence. Here is a haunting
example from the twelfth century:

Just before death, performing a ritual that
            is feudal,
I feel my frail body going limp as a noodle.
Not to worry, though. In time I will be
            reborn, possibly as a poodle.
By then mankind will have invented strudel.

The Buddha is a teacher. His instruction shows us The Way. The Buddha is a physician. His compassion heals us. The Buddha is a merciful judge. His wisdom sets us free. The Buddha is not a certified financial planner. For that you need a Supreme Being with a real head for numbers.

To practice Zen and the art of
Jewish motorcycle maintenance, do the
following: Get rid of the motorcycle.
What were you thinking?

the Buddha taught that one should practice lovingkindness to all sentient beings. Still, would it kill you to find a nice sentient being who happens to be Jewish?

happiness lies in the proper balance of good and bad, bright and dark, *yin* and *yang*. So says *The Book of Change.* You also need the proper balance of pennies, nickels, dimes, and quarters. This is covered in *The Book of Exact Change.*

One who is free from stain, well-disciplined, honest, and endowed with self-control inherits the Buddha's robe. Only one who has actually attained Nirvana is worthy of the matching slippers.

for harmonious, focused concentration, sit cross-legged, as though balancing a lotus blossom on your head, with your tailbone planted in the earth. Place your right ankle on your left thigh. Place your left ankle on your right thigh. Pull both feet in toward your kidneys. Press your knees firmly against the floor with your head upright, your chin drawn in, and your shoulders spread back. Stop screaming. If you keep scrunching up your face like that, it will stay that way.

from his high vantage point, the Buddha was able to perceive with complete clarity not just the past and the present but also the future. Practicing Zen, you, too, can begin to anticipate what others, with less elevated perspectives, cannot. Then you can say, "I told you so."

focus on your lower abdomen,
the source of all mental and bodily energy.
Ask yourself, "Why is the center of my
being called a *pupik?* And is it an innie or
an outie?"

Here, your umbilical cord physically
connected you to your mother. Her cord
connected her to her mother, and so on,
from the dawn of time. In a sense, you are
still connected and always will be. Discuss
this with your therapist.

One inch of meditation, one inch a Buddha. Inch by inch, through constant meditation, you can reach his six-foot height. Then meditate a little longer to get the waistline.

to strike his target, the Zen archer
must be conscious yet not self-conscious.
He must become one with the bow, take
aim without aiming, and let the arrow
release itself. Even after all that, it will be
a miracle if he doesn't put someone's eye
out. This raises the question "Why shoot
bows and arrows in the first place?" The
Middle Ages are over. You should find a
nice sport, like tennis.

The Lesser Vehicle is the way to attain Enlightenment for one's self. The Greater Vehicle is the way to attain Enlightenment for all people. The Sport Utility Vehicle is the way to attain four-wheel drive.

$\mathcal{E}$nter into your inner self and behold the eye of the soul. Gaze upon your original face before you were even born. Shocked? Remember, this was before the nose job.

$\mathcal{E}$ven on the road to hell, flowers can make you smile. Buy some to bring to the *mishpocha*.

Without a weapon, one does not hunt a tiger. Without a sweater, one does not dine at an air-conditioned restaurant.

just as flowers need the bees to take away their nectar, so is it necessary for you to take home the wrapped-up leftovers.

be patient and achieve all things.

Be impatient and achieve all things faster.

leave footprints like the birds in the sky. Make waves like the gefilte fish in the pond.

Those who live according to the teachings escape affliction and cross over to the farther shore. Those who do not, simply remain on this shore. Those who have truly achieved Nirvana do not remain on either this shore or the farther shore but forever leave both shores. These are not beach people.

$t$hou shalt not bow down before false idols. You may, however, rent a Buddha statue for your Zen-theme bar mitzvah.

be a light unto nations. Be a lamp unto yourself. *Shema. Om.* So long as you're in temple.

It cannot be digested. It cannot be spit out. The hot iron ball of Zen. The impenetrable matzoh ball of Judaism.

the perfume of the sandalwood, rosebay, or jasmine tree cannot travel against the wind, yet one whiff of fresh horseradish will really get up there in your sinuses.

for the weary pilgrim,

a Zen poem:

Thousands reach the gateless gate
from many paths.
Once through, they dwell serenely
between heaven and earth,
Enjoying golf, line dancing, Yiddish
lessons, and aquacise.
Come see our model units
here at Century Village.

100
=
101

The Buddha spoke of Four Abodes—the Abode of Lovingkindness, the Abode of Compassion, the Abode of Sympathetic Joy, and the Abode of Equanimity. This is far too many abodes, unless you have a lot of help. Stick to one abode, and maybe a small second abode for weekends.

Zen is not easy. It takes effort

to attain nothingness. And then what do

you have? *Bupkes.*

*e*ven the Zen hermit who dwells on a remote mountain crag amid the clouds, subsisting on roots and berries as vultures circle, should keep a coffee ring handy. What if company drops by?

The words "There is no Self" can be bewildering, even terrifying. Still, they're not as bad as "May you grow like an onion, with your head in the ground! May your bones be broken as often as the Ten Commandments! May your son's *mohel* have cataracts!"

*Y*ou have attained the goal. You are renewed by the sweet savor of newly tasted wisdom. Your features radiate intellectual power. Your eyes gleam with fresh insight. Your form shines like the moon in the night sky. Your white lab coat glows like newly fallen snow. Congratulations, medical school graduate.

The Tao has no expectations. The Tao demands nothing of others. The Tao does not speak. The Tao does not blame. The Tao does not take sides. The Tao is not Jewish.

In nature, there is no good or bad,
better or worse. The wind may blow or not.
The flowering branch grows long or short.
Do not judge or prefer. Ask only, "Is it
good for the Jews?"

$\mathcal{G}$o, then, and wander for the good of the many, for the welfare of the many, out of compassion for the world, for the benefit and happiness of gods and men. Teach the Dharma that is good in the beginning, good in the middle, and good in the end. Don't forget to write. And always wear clean underwear. You never know when you could end up in the emergency room.

the journey of a thousand miles

begins with a single *oy*.

About the Author

*d*avid M. Bader is a writer in Manhattan, where he was born and raised. Through Zen meditation, he has managed to achieve complete and perfect Emptiness, although two hours later he often feels full again.